Piano Solo

Revelation Song
& 10 More Worship Hits

Arranged by Larry Moore

ISBN 978-1-4234-9169-9

HAL•LEONARD®
CORPORATION

7777 W. BLUEMOUND RD. P.O. BOX 13819 MILWAUKEE, WI 53213

Visit Hal Leonard Online at
www.halleonard.com

BE UNTO YOUR NAME

Words and Music by LYNN DeSHAZO
and GARY SADLER

Worshipfully

FROM THE INSIDE OUT

Words and Music by
JOEL HOUSTON

DAYS OF ELIJAH

Words and Music by
ROBIN MARK

HOSANNA

Words and Music by
BROOKE FRASER

HOW HE LOVES

Words and Music by
JOHN MARK McMILLAN

Slowly, in 2

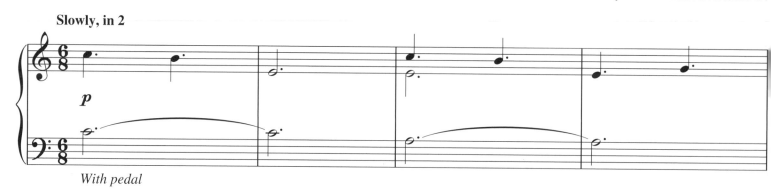

p

With pedal

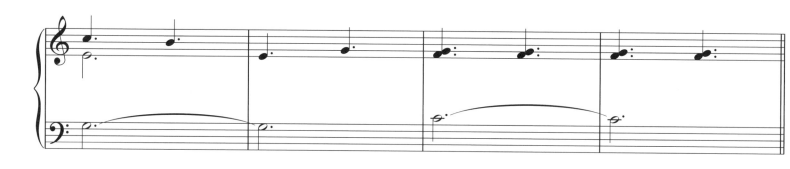

Bring out melody

LEAD ME TO THE CROSS

Words and Music by
BROOKE FRASER

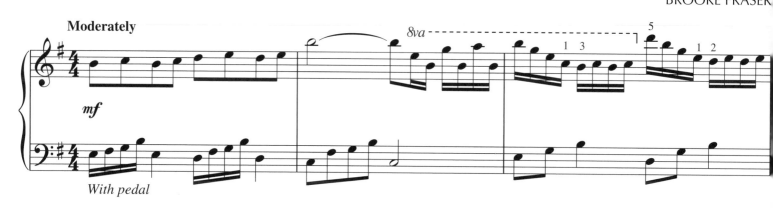

MADE ME GLAD

Words and Music by
MIRIAM WEBSTER

Moderately, with a strong pulse

mf – mp

With pedal

To Coda

OFFERING

Words and Music by
PAUL BALOCHE

REVELATION SONG

Words and Music by
JENNIE LEE RIDDLE

Moderately slow

WORTHY IS THE LAMB

Words and Music by
DARLENE ZSCHECH

Worshipfully

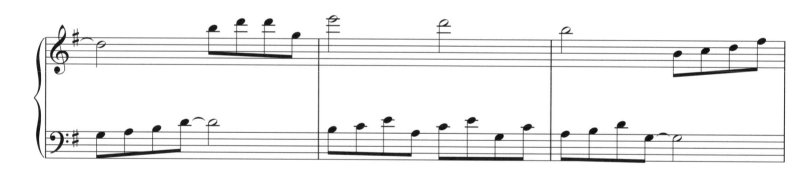

STILL

Words and Music by
REUBEN MORGAN

Reverently